TABLE PRAYERS

TABLE PRAYERS

*New Prayers,
Old Favorites,
Songs, &
Responses*

Mildred Tengbom

AUGSBURG PUBLISHING HOUSE
MINNEAPOLIS, MINNESOTA

CONTENTS

ACKNOWLEDGEMENTS

Appreciation is expressed to publishers and individuals for their permission to use material cited below. All rights are reserved by the copyright holders. Every effort has been made to locate the source and secure permission for use of copyrighted material. Inadvertent omissions, if called to the publisher's attention, will be noted in future editions. Most prayers in the sections "Prayers for Today," "Responsive Prayers," and "Prayers for Special Days," unless otherwise noted, are written by the compiler of this book.

"Thank you, God, for milk and bread," from *God's Wonderful World* by Agnes Leckie Mason and Phyllis Brown Ohanion, copyright by Agnes Leckie Mason.

"O Lord, we beseech Thee" by Lucy H. M. Soulsby, and "Father, whose life within us" by Dr. Ida Scudder, from *Prayers of Women* edited by Lisa Sergio, copyright 1965 by Lisa Sergio.

"Grandfather, Great Spirit," from *Your*

Prayers and Mine by Elizabeth Yates, copyright 1954 by Houghton Mifflin.

"For all the things for which we seldom give thanks" by Samuel H. Miller, from *Prayers for Daily Use* by Samuel H. Miller, copyright 1959 by Samuel H. Miller, by permission of Harper and Row.

"Let us praise God," from *The Kingdom, the Power and the Glory* edited by James Henry Daugherty, copyright 1933 by Oxford University Press.

Prayer from Africa, from *Sing and Pray and Shout Hurray* by Roger Ortmayer, copyright 1974 by Friendship Press.

Prayer from Italy, from *Children's Prayers Around the World* by Helen Clarke, copyright 1959 by Christian Children's Fund, Inc.

Prayers from India, Iran, and Columbia, from *Book of Children's Prayers* compiled for UNICEF by William I. Kaufman, copyright William I. Kaufman.

"O God, our loving Father," from *Letters and Miscellanies of Robert Louis Stevenson, The Thistle Edition*, Vol. 22, copyright by Charles Scribner's Sons.

"O Christ, if ever I esteem," from *Every*

Good Gift by Jane Merchant, poem copyright 1966 assigned to Abingdon Press.

"Lord God, our Father" by Karl Barth, from *Selected Prayers by Karl Barth,* copyright 1965 by M. E. Bratcher, by permission of John Knox Press.

"A circle of friends is a blessed thing" by Walter Rauschenbusch, from *Prayers of the Social Awakening* by Walter Rauschenbusch, copyright 1910 by Pilgrim Press.

"Our Father, for many years" by Robert Louis Stevenson, from *Prayers Written at Vailima* by Robert Louis Stevenson, copyright 1960 by Charles Scribner's Sons.

"Blessed Lord, who has given us the earth," from *O Worship the Lord,* by permission of Seabury Press.

"O Lord, we thank you for the privilege" by Louis Bromfield, from *Prayers of the Free Spirit* compiled by Stephen Hall Fritchman, copyright 1945 by William Morrow and Company.

Ideas for Mealtime Prayer

Prayer *does* change us. Even a few moments spent in prayer every day make a difference. According to a study cited by Billy Graham, only one out of forty marriages ends in divorce when parents attend church regularly, and only one out of four hundred when both parents with their children attend church regularly and maintain family devotions.

For many families the best time of the day to pray together is at the evening meal. Four books can help you enrich this time: a Bible, preferably in a version the children can readily understand; a hymnbook or Christian songbook; a notebook in which to enter family prayer concerns; and a book of table prayers. Read a passage from the Bible, sing or read a hymn, discuss prayer concerns, and then pray.

This book has been designed to help you during prayer time by introducing freshness and variety. Children can lead in short prayers they have memorized. All can participate in responsive prayers. Included also are prayers to sing, contemporary prayers, and prayers from times past. You will also find prayers for special occasions.

Praying together as a family requires effort and discipline, but it is well worth it. Teach religious faith to children, and in most cases they will firmly maintain it throughout life. This belief, long clung to by many of us, was substantiated by research by Dean R. Hoge of Catholic University and Larry G. Keeter of Appalachian State University. In the September 1976 issue of the *Journal of the Scientific Study of Religion,* they revealed that the widely held belief that science gradually displaces religious commitment was not sustained in their research findings. School training has little effect on religious belief instilled in childhood. Even among the most highly educated college teachers, the findings suggest, early training and family conditioning highly influence later religious beliefs and practices.

So do not despair and give up as you struggle with restless children, busy schedules, interruptions and distractions. Persevere. Prayer *does* change us.

Prayers for Small Children

Dear Father, hear us as we say
thank you for our food today. Amen.

✤

Before I eat, I bow my head
and thank you, God, for daily bread. Amen.

✤

For food we eat,
for clothes we wear,
for nightly rest
and daily care,
we thank you, heavenly Father. Amen.

✤

Come, Lord Jesus, be our Guest
and let these gifts to us be blest. Amen.

✤

Father, my hands I fold, my head I bow:
for food and drink I thank you now. Amen.

✤

Dear God,
you gave us a beautiful world.
We enjoy
swimming when it is hot,
drinking cool drinks,
running and playing,
flying kites,
walking in the rain,
eating ice cream and popcorn and pizza.
Thank you, dear God.
(Use this as a pattern. Have children suggest
what they especially like to do, and what
their favorite foods are.)

✤

Let us at this table say
a thank-you prayer for all this day,
for home and loved ones gathered here,
for all God's children everywhere. Amen.

✤

1

Thank you, God, for milk and bread;
thank you for my cozy bed;
thank you for my friends and play,
and for every happy day.

2

Thank you, God, for sunshine bright;
thank you for the stars at night;
thank you for the world so fair,
and your tender, loving care.

3

Thank you, God, for all green trees;
thank you for the gentle breeze;
thank you for the flowers in spring,
for the birds, for everything.

AGNES LECKIE MASON BEALS

✤

Dear God,
thank you for the Bible
that tells us you love us.
Thank you for this food
that shows us you love us.
Help us to love you more and more. Amen.

✤

Dear God, you love not only us, but
everyone. Help us to love those who have a
different color of skin than we do or who
speak a different language. Many of them are
hungry. Take care of them too. Thank you
for this food. Help us to share what we have
with others. Amen.

✤

Thank you, Lord, for happy hearts,
for fair and sunny weather.
Thank you, Lord, for this our food,
and that we are together. Amen.

✤

God is great and God is good,
and we thank him for this food.
By his hand we all are fed;
give us, Lord, our daily bread.
Bless our home with peace and love,
and grant in Christ a home above. Amen.

✤

Our Father,
we thank you for all the vegetables growing
in our garden. We thank you for the flowers
and the plants in our house. We thank you
for all the food we get from the supermarkets
and bakeries and dairies. We know you give
us all these good things because you love us.
Thank you, God. Amen.

✤

For food and drink, to you be praise.
Teach us by faith to keep your ways. Amen.

✤

We thank you, loving Father,
for all your tender care,
for food and clothes and shelter
and all your world so fair. Amen.

✤

For every cup and plateful,
God, make us truly grateful.

✤

Prayers for Today

Haven't we had a wonderful time around our table, Lord? The food was good. We feel much better after eating. It was good talking with each other. The warmth and encouragement of our family circle made us glad again that you have placed us in families. Best of all, you were here with us. Thank you, Lord, for a mealtime that has refreshed us. Amen.

✤

Our Father, may the strength that comes through the food you give us enable us to do your will, for Christ's sake. Amen.

✤

We thank you, Father, for the gift of friends
and for all the blessings of friendship.
We thank you for the happy hours we have
spent together the past day(s). Go with our
friends now and bring them safely back to
their home(s). Keep us all strong in
Christian love and hope and in service to
you and to one another. Amen.

✢

For this our daily food
and for every gift which comes from you,
we bless your holy name;
through Jesus Christ our Lord. Amen.

✢

Father in heaven,
sustain our bodies with this food,
our hearts with true love,
and our souls with your truth,
for Christ's sake. Amen.

✢

The Lord is our God, our Savior, our
Companion. How can we ever be lonely as
long as he is with us? This day again he
has provided for all our needs, loved us,
cared for us, and comforted us. Should all
else fail us, we know he will never abandon
us. Thanks and praise be to his holy name!

✠

Great God, who made a world that gives
to us the best of everything and who placed
within our hearts a longing for you, we lift
our hearts in praise and worship. We thank
you for all your love and mercy, and we pray
that the hour around our table may deepen
our appreciation for all you do for us. Amen.

✠

Our loving heavenly Father, as we come to
the table tonight we are tired. Some of us
have had a hard day. We know you love us
as we are. Help us to love each other as we
are. Help us to make this mealtime a time
that will help us. Help us not to argue or say
unkind things. Help us rather to know what
to say to each other that will encourage and
lift our hearts. If one of us should erupt in
anger, help us to understand that too and
forgive. Be with us, then, at our meal, and
refresh us, body, mind, and spirit; in Jesus'
name we ask it, with thanksgiving. Amen.

✢

O God, who, in the beginning of time, came
at evening to commune with your children,
we come to you now. As we sit quietly before
you, hush our spirits. Help us center our
thoughts on you.
(Sit in silence for at least 30 seconds.)
Each one of us wants to offer special thanks
to you.
(Pray in silence, each in your own heart.)
Each one of us wants to leave a care with you.
(Pray in silence.)
And now together we thank you for this
moment of communion with you, for the
haven of our home, for our loved ones
around this table, and also for the food on it.
Thank you, Father. Amen.

✤

O God, you are the giver
of every good and perfect gift.
We are aware of how easily we take
and how often we grudgingly give.
Give us the gift of grateful hearts,
that we may want to share freely with others
all you have given us. Amen.

✠

We look to you, O Lord,
for food to nourish our bodies,
for grace to strengthen our spirits,
and for love to enrich our lives. Amen.

✠

Thank you, Father, for this food
which is ours through your goodness.
Bless the persons who worked to provide it
and the persons who prepared it.
Keep us mindful of all the blessings
that come into our lives from you
and help us in turn to be blessings to others.
Amen.

✤

Great God, Thou Giver of all good,
accept our praise and bless our food.
Grace, health, and strength to us afford,
through Jesus Christ, our blessed Lord. Amen.

✤

Give us grateful hearts, our Father,
for all your mercies,
and make us mindful of the needs of others;
through Jesus Christ our Lord. Amen.

✤

Lord Jesus, the living water given to quench
the deepest thirst of our hearts, the bread of
heaven sent to give us life that will go on
forever, we thank you that you are mindful
of our earthly human needs also and that day
by day you provide for these needs, even as
you give us the gifts we need for our spirits.
We praise and thank you. Amen.

✦

Lord Jesus, we want to make room for you
at our table and in our hearts and lives.
Welcome, Lord Jesus! Amen.

✦

Our Father, it's so good to be able to come home at night! We thank you for homes that radiate love and care, loyalty and faithfulness. We thank you for what each one in our family means to our home, for *(Name family members and mention some special contribution they make to the home. Give opportunity for all family members to express personal words of appreciation.)* We pray that our love for you will grow, that when our time comes to leave this earth, we may be able to go with joy, because we are eager to be home with our heavenly Father. We pray in our Savior's name. Amen.

✣

O Lord, as we gather around our table tonight, we think of all the things we have left to do before we can go to bed. We remember all the things we did carelessly today. Thoughts and feelings tumble around within us. Good Lord, for just a moment we want to sit quietly. Help us to think of some peaceful, quiet scene. *(Pause and allow time for reflection.)* Thank you, Father, for the memory of pleasant places, and the calmness and balm remembering brings. Thank you for this good food. Help us to enjoy it, to eat slowly and calmly, knowing that eating will refresh and strengthen us for the evening ahead; in your Son's name, who came to give us rest. Amen. *(After prayer, share with each other the scenes you recalled.)*

✤

O Lord, for this our daily bread
and for every good gift
that comes from you,
we bless your holy name. Amen.

✠

For these and all our blessings,
God's holy name be praised;
through Jesus Christ our Lord. Amen.

✠

Lord, help us to receive
all things from your hand
and use them to your praise. Amen.

✠

Dear God, help me today
to watch my mouth
so what goes in
and what comes out
won't make me regret
or hang my head with shame.
But that at eve
I can say,
thank you, God,
for helping me
again today. Amen.

HILDA NELSON

✤

Dear Father, there is no way we can return
to you as much as we have received. Your
blessings and grace and love are far in excess
of anything we could ever hope to offer.
We can only humbly and gratefully receive
from your hand, and seek to praise you. But
we pray you will enable us to give generously
to those with whom we come in contact.
Help us to focus every day, not on receiving,
but on giving. Make us both conscious and
unconscious givers until at last giving will
become part of the natural response of our
hearts and lives; in Christ's name, who
teaches us to give. Amen.

✤

Father, you give so much, and we thank you
so little. Help us to see that what we call ours
is really yours for us to share with one
another. You have shown us in Jesus Christ
what it means to love. Help us to love each
other for what we are and to use for our
benefit the things you give us. Spare us,
Lord, from using the people you gave us to
love and from loving the things you want us
only to use. Amen.

✠

Master of life, help us to know
your companionship with us at this table,
that we may be strengthened,
not only by our daily bread,
but also by the bread of life. Amen.

✠

We thank you now, dear Lord,
for homes and friends and food.
Grant us strength to serve you this day
in such a way that we may
show our gratitude. Amen.

✠

Bless us, O Lord, and these your gifts
which we are about to receive;
through Christ our Lord. Amen.

✠

For the important things in life
we thank you, God.
We thank you
   for health,
   for life,
   for food,
   for shelter,
   for vigor,
   for work,
   for opportunities to love,
   for people who care,
   for forgiveness when we fail,
   for opportunities to begin each day
      with a new start.
Above all, keep alive in us
the new life we have in you,
through Jesus Christ, our Lord. Amen.

✣

We thank you, Father, for each other, for
the opportunity we have to love one another,
for the differences of personality that enrich
us, for occasions to show that we care about
each other. Forgive us our thoughtlessness
toward each other: our envious or hateful
thoughts, our hasty and unkind remarks.
Help us live together in forgiveness towards
each other, the forgiveness that we share in
Jesus Christ, our Lord. Amen.

✠

Our loving heavenly Father, you have supported us all the day long. Now the shadows are lengthening, and evening soon will fall. The feverish pace of our working day is over, although some of its tension still remains with us. We thank you for this hour around the table. Refresh us. Give us restful sleep tonight, and, at last, when we come to the end of life, give us eternal peace with you. Amen.

✤

For food and health and happy days,
accept our gratitude and praise.
In serving others, Lord, may we
repay our debt of love to Thee. Amen.

✤

For food to eat,
those who prepare it;
for health to enjoy it,
friends to share it;
we thank you, good Lord. Amen.

✤

You have promised
to supply our every need, Lord.
May we never doubt your love nor forget
to thank you for your faithfulness,
through Christ, our Lord. Amen.

✤

Lord Jesus, be our holy guest,
our morning joy, our evening rest,
and with our daily bread impart
your love and peace to every heart. Amen.

*(May be sung
to Old Hundredth
or Tallis' Canon)*

✤

O Lord God, how generously you have
lavished beauty on our earth! How
abundantly you have provided for us! We
have all we need, and more—much, much
more. Forgive us when we become envious
when others have things we want but do not
need. Help us to be truly grateful for all we
have. Give us contented hearts. We receive
this food you have given us with
thanksgiving.

✤

O Father, make our praise
as constant as your love toward us. Amen.

✤

Prayers from Times Past

Grandfather, Great Spirit, you have been always, and before you nothing has been. There is no one to pray to but you. The star nations all over the heavens are yours, and yours are the grasses of the earth. You are older than all need, older than all pain and prayer. Grandfather, Great Spirit, fill us with the light. Give us the strength to understand and the eyes to see. Teach us to walk the soft earth as relatives to all that live. Help us, for without you we are nothing.

Sioux Indian Prayer

✤

Let us in peace eat the food
God has provided for us.
Praise be to God for all his gifts. Amen.

✤

May the abundance of this table
never fail and never be less,
thanks to the blessings of God,
who has fed us and satisfied our needs.
To him be glory for ever. Amen.

✤

*(The first of these two ancient prayers of
the Armenian Apostolic Church is to be
said before meals, and the second after
meals.)*

Give us, Lord, a bit o' sun,
a bit o' work and a bit o' fun;
give us all in the struggle and sputter
our daily bread and a bit o' butter;
give us health, our keep to make,
an' a bit to spare for others' sake;
give us sense, for we're some of us duffers,
an' a heart to feel for all that suffers;
give us, too, a bit of a song
and a tale, and a book to help us along.
An' give us our share o' sorrow's lesson
that we may prove how grief's a blessin'.
Give us, Lord, a chance to be
our goodly best, brave, wise, and free,
our goodly best for ourself, and others,
till all men learn to live as brothers.

(From the wall of an old inn,
Lancaster, England)

✤

Let (us) thank the Lord
for his steadfast love,
for his wonderful works to the sons of men!
For he satisfies him who is thirsty,
and the hungry he fills with good things.
                              Psalm 107:8-9

✦

O Lord, we beseech Thee to bless and
prosper this Thy household. Grant us sweet
reasonableness in all our dealings with one
another. Make us large-hearted in helping
and generous in criticizing; keep us from
unkind words and from unkind silences.
Make us quick to understand the needs and
feelings of others; and grant that living in the
brightness of Thy presence we may bring
sunshine into cloudy places.
                              LUCY H.M. SOULSBY

✦

Great art Thou, O Lord,
and greatly to be praised.
Great is Thy power,
and of Thy wisdom there is no number,
And man desires to praise Thee.
He is but a tiny part
of all that Thou hast created;
Yet this tiny part desires to praise Thee,
Thou dost so excite him
that to praise Thee is his joy.
For Thou hast made us for Thyself,
And our hearts are restless
till they rest in Thee.

Augustine, *Africa*
Fifth Century

✤

Give us, O Lord, thankful hearts
which never forget your goodness to us.
Give us, O Lord, grateful hearts,
which do not waste time complaining.
Give us, O Lord, steadfast hearts,
which no unworthy affections
may drag downwards;
Give us, O Lord, unconquered hearts,
which no tribulation can wear out.
Give us, O Lord, upright hearts,
which no unworthy purpose may tempt aside.

ST. THOMAS AQUINAS *(Adapted)*

✤

Father, whose life is within us and whose love is ever about us, grant that your life may be maintained in our lives today and every day as with gladness of heart, without haste or confusion of thought, we go about our daily tasks, conscious of ability to meet every rightful demand, seeing the larger meaning of little things, and finding beauty and love everywhere. In the sense of your presence may we walk through the hours, breathing the atmosphere of love rather than anxious striving. To this end we receive with gratitude and thanksgiving this meal which you give us for refreshment and strength.

DR. IDA SCUDDER *(Adapted)*

✤

O Lord our God,
without whose will and pleasure
not a sparrow can fall to the ground,
grant to us in times of trouble
to be patient without murmuring or despair,
and in prosperity to acknowledge Thy gifts,
and to confess that
all our endowments come from Thee.
O Father of lights,
who givest liberally and upbraidest not,
give us, by Thy Holy Spirit,
a willing heart and a ready hand
to use all Thy gifts
to Thy praise and glory;
through Jesus Christ our Lord.

ARCHBISHOP CRANMER

✤

O Lord,
give us
more love,
more self-denial,
more kindness to Thee.
Make us
kindly in thought,
gentle in word,
generous in deed.
Teach us that it is better
to give than to receive,
to forget ourselves
than to put ourselves forward,
to minister than to be ministered unto.
Unto Thee, the God of love,
be all the glory and praise,
both now and for evermore. Amen.

DEAN HENRY ALFORD
19th century theologian

✳

The blessings of God rest upon all those who
have been kind to us, have cared for us,
have worked for us, have served us, and have
shared our bread with us at this table. Our
merciful God, reward all of them in Thy own
way, for Thine is the glory and the honor
forever. Amen.

SAINT CYRIL OF EGYPT

✤

We praise Thee for Thy blessings.
Teach us, good Lord,
to serve Thee as Thou deservest;
to give and not to count the cost;
to fight and not to heed the wounds;
to toil and not to seek for rest;
to labor and not to ask for any reward
save that of knowing that we do Thy will,
through Jesus Christ, our Lord. Amen.

IGNATIUS LOYOLA

✤

As we go into a new day
we thank Thee for all Thy mercies,
for the refreshment of sleep and food,
and we beseech Thee that this day
Thy strength would pilot us,
Thy power preserve us,
Thy wisdom instruct us,
Thy eye watch over us,
Thy ear hear us,
Thy Word give us sweet talk,
Thy hand defend us, and
Thy way guide us.

ST. PATRICK *(Adapted)*

✤

Clap your hands, all peoples! *(Clap.)*
Shout to God with loud songs of joy!
(Shout "Hallelujah!")
Sing praises to God, sing praises!
Sing praises to our King, sing praises!
For God is the king of all the earth;
sing praises with a psalm!

> *Psalm 47:1, 6, 7*

✤

I will sing of thy steadfast love,
O Lord, for ever;
with my mouth I will proclaim
thy faithfulness to all generations.
For thy steadfast love
was established for ever,
thy faithfulness is firm as the heavens.

> *Psalm 89:1-2*

✤

O Lord, we thank you
for the privilege and gift of living
in a world filled with beauty
and excitement and variety.
We thank you
for the gift of loving and being loved,
for the friendliness and understanding
and beauty of animals
on the farm and in the forest,
for the green of trees
and sound of a waterfall,
the darting beauty
of the trout in the brook.
We thank you for all the senses
you have bestowed upon us
and for the delights they bring us.
We thank you for our bodies which are
such wonderful and delightful mechanisms.
We thank you for making eating so enjoyable
and food so delectable.
We thank you
for all these things and many more,
and most of all for life itself,
without which the universe
would have no meaning. Amen.

LOUIS BROMFIELD

✤

Blessed Lord,
who has given us the earth to live upon,
warmed by the sun,
made wet by the rain,
with fields and gardens and orchards;
help us to use these good things fairly,
and with kindness toward one another,
working for each other,
and living for you.
Glory be to you, O Lord. Amen.

✤

Bless the Lord, O my soul;
and all that is within me,
bless his holy name!
Bless the Lord, O my soul,
and forget not all his benefits.
Psalm 103:1-2

✤

Give me a good digestion, Lord,
and also something to digest;
give me a healthy body, Lord,
with sense to keep it at its best.
Give me a healthy mind, good Lord,
to keep the pure and good in sight,
which seeing sin is not appalled
but finds a way to set it right;
give me a mind that is not bored,
that does not whimper, whine or sigh;
don't let me worry overmuch
about the fussy thing called I.
(Found in Chester Cathedral, England)

✦

We thank you, our Father,
that you have been with us this day.
In a few hours we shall go to bed.
Go with each of us to rest.
If any awake,
make the dark hours of watching endurable.
When day returns,
return to us,
our Sun and Comforter.
Call us up
with morning faces
and morning hearts,
eager to work,
eager to be happy,
if happiness should be our portion,
and if the day be marked for sorrow,
make us strong to endure it. Amen.

ROBERT LOUIS STEVENSON.

✤

Make a joyful noise to the Lord,
all the lands!
Serve the Lord with gladness!
Come into his presence with singing!
Know that the Lord is God!
It is he that made us, and we are his;
we are his people,
and the sheep of his pasture.
Enter his gates with thanksgiving,
and his courts with praise!
Give thanks to him, bless his name!
For the Lord is good;
his steadfast love endures for ever,
and his faithfulness to all generations.

Psalm 100

✤

Responsive Prayers

Every time we have a meal and think of
God's love, we grow in inner strength; and
as God makes us healthy in body through the
food we eat, we pray that he may give us
food for our souls. God be in my head,
    R/ and in my understanding.
God be in mine eyes,
    R/ and in my looking.
God be in my mouth,
    R/ and in my speaking.
God be in my heart,
    R/ and in my thinking.
God be in this meal,
    R/ and in my eating.
God be in mine all
    R/ till my departing.

God, our heavenly Father, created our world.
He sustains it and nourishes and cares for
his children. Let us praise his name.
O Lord, the rain falls, earth thaws;

R/ *Holy and blessed is your name!*

The sun shines; crops sprout and grow;

R/ *Holy and blessed is your name!*

Farmers toil, grocers stock the food
that crowns our table;

R/ *Holy and blessed is your name!*

Parents work, children help;

R/ *Holy and blessed is your name!*

Rest and relaxation await us
at the end of our day;

R/ *Holy and blessed is your name!*

You love, we love, others love;

R/ *Holy and blessed is your name!*

✤

Down through the centuries, God, you have
provided for your people and your creatures.
Great is your faithfulness, O God! As you
gave the plants of the fields and the fruits
of the trees to our first parents,

R/ So you give us food to eat, O Lord.
As you provided for Noah
and his family in the ark,

R/ So you give us food to eat, O Lord.
As you sent quail and manna to the Israelites
as they traveled in the desert wilderness,

R/ So you give us food to eat, O Lord.
As you declared that the oxen who thresh
the grains should be given grain to eat,

R/ So you give us food to eat, O Lord.
As you fed the hungry multitudes
and provided for your disciples,

R/ So you give us food to eat, O Lord.
Great is your faithfulness, O God, our Father.
You do not change. Your compassions do not
fail. We worship and adore you. We praise
and thank you.

✠

We thank you for your promises,
O God, our Father:
"So don't worry at all about having enough
food and clothing . . . your heavenly Father
already knows perfectly well that you need
them, and he will give them to you if you
give him first place in your life and live as he
wants you to." (Matt. 6:31-33 LB)

   R/ We thank you for your promises, Lord.
"Give generously, for your gifts will return to
you later." (Eccles. 11:1 LB)

   R/ We thank you for your promises, Lord.
"Don't worry about anything; instead, pray
about everything; tell God your needs and
don't forget to thank him for his answers. . . .
And it is he who will supply all your needs
from his riches in glory, because of what
Christ Jesus has done for us." (Phil. 4:6, 19 LB)

   R/ We thank you for your promises, Lord.
"God is able to provide you with every
blessing in abundance, so that you may
always have enough of everything and may
provide in abundance for every good work.
. . . He who supplies seed to the sower and

bread for food will supply and multiply your
resources and increase the harvest of your
righteousness." (2 Cor. 9:8, 10)
   R/ *We thank you for your promises, Lord.*
Now to our Creator God, our heavenly
Father, who has promised never to abandon
us as orphans but to care for us all our lives,
and who has promised to bless and use what
we share, be honor, praise, respect, and
appreciation. Amen.

✤

Dear Heavenly Father,
We thank you for food,
   R/ *and remember the hungry.*
We thank you for health,
   R/ *and remember the sick.*
We thank you for friends,
   R/ *and remember the friendless.*
We thank you for freedom,
   R/ *and remember the enslaved.*
May these remembrances help us
use your gifts for others also. Amen.

✤

Bless the Lord, O my soul;
and all that is within me,
bless his holy name!
O God, for all you've done for us,
    R/ we thank you, yes, thank you.
For your provision of our every need,
    R/ we thank you, yes, thank you.
For our families,
who sometimes we take for granted,
    R/ we thank you, yes, thank you.
For the work we've done today,
for its disciplines, its satisfaction,
its opportunity to serve others;
    R/ we thank you, yes, thank you.
For this hour when we can relax and enjoy
food and family and good conversation;
    R/ we thank you, yes, thank you.
Thank you for it all,
loving Father, tender Savior,
and comforting Holy Spirit.

✤

1

For flowers that bloom about our feet,
   R/ Father, we thank Thee;
For tender grass so fresh and sweet,
   R/ Father, we thank Thee;
For song of bird and hum of bee,
For all things fair we hear or see,
   R/ Father in heaven, we thank Thee.

2

For blue of stream and blue of sky,
   R/ Father, we thank Thee;
For pleasant shade of branches high,
   R/ Father, we thank Thee;
For fragrant air and cooling breeze,
For beauty of the blooming trees,
   R/ Father in heaven, we thank Thee.

3

For this new morning with its light,
   R/ Father, we thank Thee;
For rest and shelter of the night,
   R/ Father, we thank Thee;
For health and food, for love and friends,
For everything Thy goodness sends,
   R/ Father in heaven, we thank Thee.

RALPH WALDO EMERSON

✤

Praise the Lord! Bless the Lord; praise and
adore and magnify him evermore. For work
and the health and strength to do it,
> R/ *we thank you, O Lord.*

For the shapes of the hills and the trees;
for the colors of flowers and of the sea;
and for sight to enjoy them,
> R/ *we thank you, O Lord.*

For the sound of music and the laughter of
children, and for hearing to enjoy them,
> R/ *we thank you, O Lord.*

For books of all ages, for poems and songs
and for a sound mind to enjoy them,
> R/ *we thank you, O Lord.*

For home-love, for mother-love, for
father-love, for child-love, for the handclasp
of a friend,
> R/ *we thank you, O Lord.*

For your abundant provision for our every
need and your unfaltering faithfulness,
> R/ *we thank you, O Lord.*

Glory be to the Father, to the Son, and to the
Holy Spirit. Amen.

✣

For all the things for which we seldom give
thanks to you, O Lord, we humbly bow our
hearts. For common things of earth which
sustain our bodies in health and strength,
though we pay scant attention to them,
   R/ *we give you thanks.*
For far-off things in ages past or in lands
distant from us which enlarge our heritage,
expand our horizon and even improve our
health,
   R/ *we give you thanks.*
For things of the spirit which disclose to us
the beauty of your holiness and sanctify the
passing time with eternal meaning,
   R/ *we give you thanks.*
For things bought with a great price, given
us without cost, by which we are deepened
and heightened to the measure of Christ our
Lord,
   R/ *we give you thanks.*
Though there be no end to your gifts, help us
to number them as they are revealed to us
day by day. Amen.

SAMUEL H. MILLER

✣

Let us praise God for our food, and the pleasures God has given us in it. Lest we should neglect the needs of life, may he help us to shun all waste and to rejoice in sharing with others.

R/ God be praised for our food.

For the shelter from wind and weather, which hallowed by love becomes our home; may he strengthen our will that no one shall go hungry or ill-housed or ill-clad.

R/ God be praised for our home.

For our fathers and mothers, by whom he orders lives and comforts hearts, bringing strength to a house and sweetness to labor; may he hallow their work and direct their ways.

R/ God be praised for good fathers and mothers.

For the gift of children; may he help us to train them to be reverent and truthful, that they may gladden our hearts and bring joy to the world.

R/ God be praised for children.

For mirth that unites us with others and

refreshes us for our work; may he help us to
keep it kind and true.

R/ God be praised for mirth.

For health, bringing wholesomeness of body
and mind; may he help us to give our
strength to his service.

R/ God be praised for health.

Let us praise God for life.

R/ All praise be to God! Amen.

✤

O give thanks to the Lord,
for he is good,

*R/ for his steadfast love
endures for ever.*

It is he who remembered us
in our low estate,

*R/ for his steadfast love
endures for ever;*

He who gives food to all flesh,

*R/ for his steadfast love
endures for ever.*

O give thanks to the God of heaven,

*R/ for his steadfast love
endures for ever.*

From Psalm 136

✤

The Lord is faithful to his promises,
and good in all he does.
> *R/ He helps all who are in trouble;*
> *he raises all who are humbled.*

All living things look hopefully to him,
and he gives them food when they need it.
> *R/ He gives them enough*
> *and satisfies the needs of all.*

The Lord is righteous in all he does,
merciful in all his acts.
> *R/ He is near to all who call to him,*
> *who call to him with sincerity.*

He supplies the needs of all who fear him;
he hears their cry and saves them.
> *R/ I will always praise the Lord;*
> *let all creatures*
> *praise his holy name forever!*

Glory to the Father, and to the Son,
and to the Holy Spirit:
> *R/ As it was in the beginning, is now,*
> *and will be forever. Amen.*

From Psalm 145 TEV

✠

It is fitting and right that all creation
praise and worship Almighty God.
O, all you works of the Lord,
bless you the Lord:

> R/ *Praise him, and magnify him forever.*

O, you showers and dew,
bless you the Lord:

> R/ *Praise him, and magnify him forever.*

O, you winter and summer,
bless you the Lord:

> R/ *Praise him, and magnify him forever.*

O, all you green things upon the earth,
bless you the Lord:

> R/ *Praise him, and magnify him forever.*

O, all you beasts and cattle,
bless you the Lord:

> R/ *Praise him, and magnify him forever.*

O, all you members of our family,
bless you the Lord:

> R/ *Praise him, and magnify him forever.*

Praised be God! Honor and glory and praise
and love be ever and ever given to him!

❖

❧❧❧

Prayers from Other Lands

AFRICA
We are happy
because you have accepted us, dear Lord.
Sometimes we do not know what to do
with all our happiness.
We swim in your grace
like a whale in the ocean.
The saying goes:
"An ocean never dries up,"
but we know your grace also never fails.
This food you have given us
is one more proof.
Dear Lord,
your grace is our happiness.
Hallelujah!

✤

ITALY
Lord, bless our meal
As we partake
Of fruits of land and sea
And let them make us strong and well
The better to serve Thee.

✤

INDIA

We love our God
And sing his praises every day
   who has made the sun and the moon,
   and sprinkled twinkling stars in the sky.
We love our God
   who has created this universe with oceans,
   mountains and rivers,
   who has made beautiful flowers bloom,
   and bountiful trees bear sweet fruit.
We love our God
   who has taught sweet songs to the birds
   and melodious humming to the honeybee,
   who is the giver of wisdom, knowledge and
     strength,
   and the beacon light to show us the right
     path.
We love our God
   who showers his love
   and blessings on children
   and makes them intelligent and good.

✤

NORWAY

Here at the table, Lord, we bow,
to receive the food Thou dost bestow,
all to Thy honor, and for our good;
now bless in Jesus' name our food. Amen.

> *Translated by*
> PASTOR BERNHARD GULDSETH

✤

IRAN

O God, we have dedicated our hearts to you,
For we have no other refuge in the world.
Provide us with the strength we need
to do our daily tasks.
Let us be ambitious and willing to work.
Let us be pleasing to our mothers,
and obedient to our fathers.
Guide us along the path
that will bring honor to our country
so that our earnest endeavors
and our hard work
shall bring prosperity to this, our land.
Amen.

✤

EGYPT

The blessing of God rest upon all those
who have been kind to us,
have cared for us,
have worked for us,
have served us,
and have shared our bread with us
at this table.
Our merciful God,
reward all of them in your own way
for yours is the glory
and the honor forever. Amen.

> SAINT CYRIL
> Coptic Orthodox Church

✤

GERMANY

Feed us, Father, we are your children.
Comfort the sorrowing sinner.
Bless the food we have before us
that it may soul and body nourish
till with the saints we are able
to surround your banquet table.

✤

COLOMBIA
We all worship you, O God,
for all that we owe you.
Watch over those we love.
For our mother, for our father,
for our brothers and sisters,
we pray
that you will keep them long years
in health, strength, and happiness.
Give solace to the sad
and health to the sick
and bread to the needy
and to the orphan, protection and a roof.
We all worship you, O God,
for all that we owe you.

✤

IRELAND
O God, make us able
for what's on the table! Amen.

✤

Prayers to Sing

FATHER, WE THANK THEE FOR THE NIGHT

Attr. to Rebecca J. Weston

Daniel Batchellor

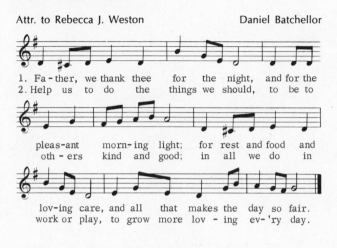

1. Fa-ther, we thank thee for the night, and for the pleas-ant morn-ing light; for rest and food and lov-ing care, and all that makes the day so fair.
2. Help us to do the things we should, to be to oth-ers kind and good; in all we do in work or play, to grow more lov-ing ev-'ry day.

HEAVENLY FATHER, KIND AND GOOD

Eoline Kowierschke

Katholisches Gesangbuch, 1774

Heav-en-ly Fa-ther, kind and good, thanks we of-fer for this food; for thy love and ten-der care, for the bless-ings that we share.

LORD JESUS, BE OUR HOLY GUEST

Thomas Tallis

Lord Je - sus, be our ho - ly guest, our morn-ing joy, our eve-ning rest; and with our dai - ly bread im-part thy love and peace to ev - 'ry heart.

ALL GOOD GIFTS AROUND US

Matthias Claudius
tr. Jane Montgomery Campbell, alt.   Johann A. P. Schulz

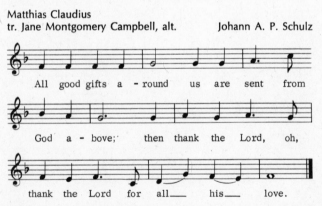

All good gifts a - round us are sent from God a - bove; then thank the Lord, oh, thank the Lord for all__ his__ love.

From *Young Children Sing,*
Lutheran Church Press and Augsburg Publishing House.

IN THY LOVE

Mary Youngman Wilson

Adapted by Lowell Mason, 1845
from Hans Georg Naegeli, 1773-1836

We thank thee, dear - est Lord, for bless - ings
from a - bove. Give us this day our dai - ly
bread and keep us in thy love.____

OH GOD IS GOOD

African

Oh, God is good. Yes, God is good.

Oh, God is good. He's so good to me.

This melody may be used to express what has happened to different family members during the course of the day. For example, these sentences can be sung:

He gives me food.　　He gives me work.
He meets my needs.　　He cheers me up.
He bears my pain.

PRAISE AND THANKSGIVING

Paraphrase of the German   Alsatian Round

Praise and thanks-giv - ing let ev - 'ry - one bring

un - to our Fa - ther for ev - 'ry good thing!

All   to - geth - er   joy - ful - ly   sing!

BE PRESENT AT OUR TABLE, LORD

John Cennick, alt.   Louis Bourgeois

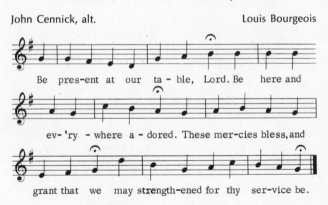

Be pres-ent at our ta - ble, Lord. Be   here and

ev - 'ry - where a - dored. These mer-cies bless, and

grant that we   may strength-ened for thy ser-vice be.

FEED THY CHILDREN

tr. Harry P. Long   Johann Crüger, 1598-1662

Feed thy chil-dren, Fa - ther ho - ly; Com-fort
let thy bless-ing now be spo - ken on the

sin - ners, poor and low-ly;
bread be - fore us bro-ken; that it serve us while we're

liv - ing, health and strength to each one giv - ing,

till at last with saints we're a - ble

to sur - round thy heav'n-ly ta - ble.

GOD LOVES ME, HE GIVES ME FOOD

M.O.   Mother Mary Oswin

God loves me   and   he gives me food and   ver-y good
food he gives. It makes me   big   and   it makes me
strong   and my bod - y   grows and   lives.   If   he
did-n't   give   me food   I   would die, die, die; I would
sim-ply fade a - way.   So   I'll tell him now that I'm
ver - y   glad that   he   loves me so   to - day.

COME WITH HEARTS REJOICING

Lina A. Rauschenberg, alt.   Casper Ett

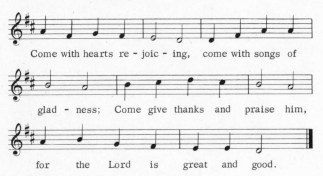

Come with hearts re - joic - ing, come with songs of glad - ness; Come give thanks and praise him, for the Lord is great and good.

GOD THE FATHER BLESS US

Charles R. Anders

God the Fa-ther bless us, God the Son pro - tect us, God the Spir - it keep us— now and ev-er-more.

PSALM 89

Psalm 89:1 KJV

I will sing of the mer-cies of the Lord for-
ev - er. I will sing,___ I will sing.___
I will sing of the mer-cies of the Lord for-
ev - er, I will sing of the mer-cies of the Lord.
___ With my mouth___ will I make known___ thy
faith - ful - ness,___ thy faith - ful - ness.___
With my mouth will I make known thy faith-ful-
ness to all gen-er - a - tions. I will sing

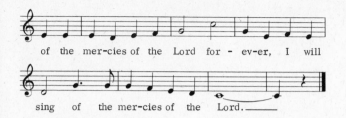

of the mer-cies of the Lord for - ev-er, I will

sing of the mer-cies of the Lord.___

From *Jesus Style Songs*, Vol. 1, Augsburg Publishing House.

COME AND DINE

C.B.W.   C. B. Widmeyer

"Come and dine," the Mas - ter call - eth, "Come and dine;"

you may feast at Je - sus' ta - ble all the time.

He who fed the mul - ti-tude, turned the wa - ter in-to

wine, to the hun- gry call - eth now, "Come and dine."

THANKS WE OFFER

Eoline Kowierschke

John Edgar Gould, 1822-75

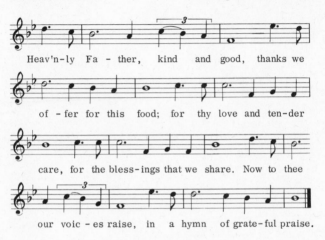

Heav'n-ly Fa - ther, kind and good, thanks we of - fer for this food; for thy love and ten-der care, for the bless-ings that we share. Now to thee our voic - es raise, in a hymn of grate-ful praise.

FOR HEALTH AND STRENGTH

(May be sung as a round.)

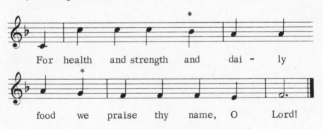

For health and strength and dai - ly food we praise thy name, O Lord!

WE THANK THEE, LORD

Mary Youngman Wilson   Wilhelm A. F. Schulthes, 1816-79

We thank thee, Lord, for dai-ly food, for dai-ly love and care;— Help us to use these gifts of grace to serve you ev-'ry-where.—

TO GOD WHO GIVES US DAILY BREAD

Mary Rumsey   Thomas Tallis

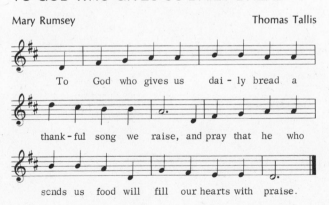

To God who gives us dai-ly bread a thank-ful song we raise, and pray that he who sends us food will fill our hearts with praise.

SCOTTISH GRACE

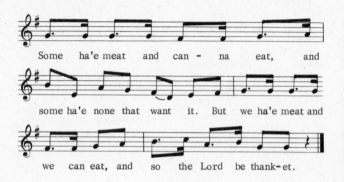

Some ha'e meat and can - na eat, and
some ha'e none that want it. But we ha'e meat and
we can eat, and so the Lord be thank- et.

I FOLD MY HANDS, I BOW MY HEAD

Agnes Louise Dean   Edward B. Birge

I fold my hands, I bow my head
to thank thee, God, for this good bread.

Music from *New Music Horizons*, First Book,
copyright 1944 Silver Burdett Co. Used by permission.

THANK YOU FOR THE WORLD SO SWEET

Edith Rutter Leatham

Jonathan Battishill

Thank you for the world so sweet; thank you for the food we eat; thank you for the birds that sing; thank you, God, for ev-'ry-thing.

From *Young Children Sing*, copyright 1967
Lutheran Church Press and Augsburg Publishing House.
Words copyright by Mrs. Lorna Hill, Cumberland, England.

Prayers for Special Days

ADVENT

Dear heavenly Father,
thank you for the happy days of Advent when
we get ready to celebrate Jesus' birthday.
Thank you for sending Jesus to earth to live
and die for us. As we light the Advent
candles, we thank you for all your care for
us. Thank you also for this food. Amen.

✠

CHRISTMAS

Dear God, thank you for our Christmas tree,
for the presents we get,
and for the Christmas cookies and goodies.
But thank you most of all for baby Jesus.
Amen.

✠

CHRISTMAS

Our heavenly Father, we thank you for this
food and that we can be together to eat it.
We rejoice that you too are with us.
We thank you that in the person of your Son
you came to this earth. What a difference
it has made for us, Lord! Now all life is
full with new meaning and beauty. We thank
and praise you. Amen.

✠

CHRISTMAS

O God, our loving Father, help us rightly to
remember the birth of Jesus that we may
share in the song of the angels, the gladness
of the shepherds, and the worship of the
wise men. Close the door of hate and open
the door of love all over the world. Let
kindness come with every gift and good
desire with every greeting. Deliver us from
evil by the blessing that Christ brings, and
teach us to be merry with clear hearts.
May the Christmas morning make us happy
to be thy children, and the Christmas evening
bring us to our beds with grateful thoughts,
forgiving and forgiven for Jesus' sake. Amen.

ROBERT LOUIS STEVENSON

✤

THE NEW YEAR

May we look into the new year
with anticipation,
grateful for the past,
ready to serve you in the future.
Thank you for this meal
and for all your blessings to us. Amen.

MINNIE C. HERMANSON

✤

GOOD FRIDAY

O Christ, if ever I esteem
the place where I am serving
too lowly for me; if I deem
another undeserving,
let me remember Thee, O Son
of God, let faith behold Thee
bending to bathe the feet of one
who had already sold Thee.

JANE MERCHANT

✣

EASTER

Lord God, our Father, you are the life which
mocks at death, and you have opened the
access to such life to us also. In Jesus Christ,
your Son, our brother, you have done all
this. We are all of us very small Christians
and not great ones. But your grace is
sufficient for us. Make us aware therefore
of the little joy and thankfulness of which
we are capable, of the timid faith we are
able to muster, of the incomplete obedience
which we cannot refuse and thereby of the
hope for the great, the whole, the complete
work which you have prepared for us all
in the death of our Lord Jesus Christ and
promised in his resurrection from the dead.
In that hope our family wants to celebrate
Easter this day, as we praise and worship
you. Amen.

KARL BARTH *(Adapted)*

✣

MEMORIAL DAY

Dear God, today we remember all who have died in wars. We pray that you would teach us to live peaceably with each other at home, at school, and at work so wars will not have to happen. Teach us to settle disputes in other ways than by fighting. Help us not to plan evil against anyone. If anyone harms us in any way, keep us from hurting them. Enable us to forgive. Help us to reconcile friends who are angry with one another. Teach us to listen to others, to respect their opinions, and to consider how they feel. Give wisdom to all the rulers of nations. Set us free from selfishness and help us to love those in need and to share with them what we have. Care for all those who suffer because of wars or famine, oppression or discrimination. In Jesus' name, who came to bring peace. Amen.

✤

MOTHER'S DAY

Loving heavenly Father, we thank you for
our mothers and grandmothers and all they
have meant and mean to us. We thank you
that they daily work to make our lives
rich and rewarding and our home a
comfortable place. We thank you for their
faith and example. We thank you that most
of the time they are patient and
understanding and that they always forgive
us. We thank you for their confidence in
us and for their encouragement. We thank
you for your abundant forgiveness when
they, like us, stumble and sin. Provide for
them opportunities to grow intellectually,
emotionally, and spiritually. Help us
understand how we can show our love for
them in meaningful ways, and may we never
take them for granted. In Jesus' name we
pray. Amen.

✤

FATHER'S DAY

Dear God, we thank you for our fathers and grandfathers. We thank you for their willingness to work so our lives can be rich and happy, offering many opportunities. We thank you for their thought and concern about our future and for the plans they make. We thank you for their love, their patience, their belief in us, their forgiveness and their desire to help. We ask that you give them daily strength, enjoyable work, and assurance that you will always help them. We pray that our family might live so our fathers can be proud of us and so they will feel all they have sacrificed for our sakes has been worthwhile. Give them joy and peace of heart and mind and a satisfying sense of fulfillment. In Jesus' name. Amen.

✛

SEEDTIME

O God of the springtime! God of the thawing
earth, the rushing streams, the quiet showers,
God of the birds winging their way north,
the bees and insects that will pollinate, the
sun that will quicken and nourish life—we
praise you! We pray for pregnant seeds
being sown now in fields. If it be your will,
give us a favorable year and good harvest
so not only we shall be fed, but the hungry
of other lands as well. Thank you for your
care for us through the winter and for our
daily bread. Amen.

✛

GRADUATION

Our Father, we thank you for having brought
————— to the successful completion of
this period of study. We pray that you would
give ————— understanding to know what
to do, courage to do it, patience to acquire
necessary skills, perseverance to accomplish
goals, strength to resist the temptation to
settle for second best. Father, help —————
to begin, to continue, and to end all things
in you. Amen.

✛

WHEN RAIN IS NEEDED

O God, our Creator and Sustainer, you who
tilt the water jars of heaven, you who shout
to clouds to release rain, you who provide
for even the crows when their young in the
nest gape for hunger, as your children we
come to you. Look with compassion and pity
upon us, your children, and our parched
fields. Father, the crops are dying. If it be
your will, cause it to rain so the crops we
have sown and cared for may grow and
produce food for us and for those whom we,
through our labor, feed. We are utterly
dependent on you. We cast ourselves on your
mercy, bold in making our request because
we do so in the name of our Savior, your
Son, the Lord Jesus. Amen.

✣

LABOR DAY

O God, you who have given to us work to
express ourselves and to provide for our
needs and the needs of those we love, we
come to you today to pray for all workers.
For those who toil in the heat of the day,
on farms, in industries, on construction and
maintenance jobs, we pray that they may
receive fair wages and satisfaction from work
well done. Help us to be grateful for the
vast multitudes at work to make life pleasant
for us.

  R/ We seek your help, O God.
For all who are in authority over others,
we pray that you would save them from
selfish ambitions. Give them concern for all
who work with them. For the rulers of our
nations, we ask wisdom, humility, restraint,
and a spirit of servanthood.

  R/ We seek your help, O God.
For teachers, for pastors and other spiritual
instructors, we ask a personal concern for
those they teach, a desire to develop
character as well as impart knowledge, and
a dedication to the truth. We pray that

their lives will be models of an honorable
way of life.
  R/ *We seek your help, O God.*
O Creator God, may our work be in tune with
nature. Enlighten us so our work will not
destroy the resources you have placed for us
in the earth. Lead us to consider the needs
of the generations to follow. Give us
thankful hearts and contentment with less
so others may have more.
  R/ *We seek your help, O God. Amen.*

✠

VETERANS' DAY

We give thanks to you, Father God, for all
the good things this land, our country has
given to us and continues to offer us. Help
us never to forget that many of these
blessings have been bought and paid for by
human sacrifice. Help us never to lightly
regard these blessings, but instead to be
grateful for those who in years past labored
and loved, suffered, became crippled, or died
so we might have something to inherit. We
pray in humbleness and thanksgiving. Amen.

✠

THANKSGIVING

For all the blessings of a great land, O Lord, we give you humble thanks and praise your name! For rich farmlands, for prairies broad and beautiful, for mountains that crown our land with snow-capped majesty, and for the mighty oceans that thunder in along our coasts, we praise you, Lord. But most of all, for freedom and opportunity and bountiful provision of all our needs, we thank you.

✤

WHEN GUESTS DINE WITH US

A circle of friends is a blessed thing.
Sweet is the breaking of bread with friends.
For the honor of their presence at our board
we are deeply grateful. Amen.

WALTER RAUSCHENBUSCH

✤

Thanks be to Thee for friendship shared,
Thanks be to Thee for food prepared.
Bless Thou the cup; bless Thou the bread;
Thy blessing rest upon each head.

✤

NATIONAL HOLIDAY

Lord, once more we lift up our voices in
praise and thanksgiving, for all the renewed
mercies which we experience at Thy hand.
We thank Thee that Thou hast placed us
in that portion of all earth in which we may
enjoy so great a measure of personal comfort,
and are, at the same time, favoured with
so great advantages for our everlasting
happiness. We thank Thee that we enjoy
liberty of person and security of substance,
and pass day after day in abundance and
peace. O let us remember the obligations
which rest upon us, and be filled with more
continual gratitude to Thee, our great and
unwearied Benefactor.

WILLIAM WILBERFORCE

❖

WHEN CROPS ARE DESTROYED

Our Father, our hearts are crushed. We thought we would have bountiful crops and now all has been wiped out. We don't know how to pray. In our despair we cry out to you. Put your arms around us. Encourage us. Love us. Comfort us. Help us to think about, not what we have lost, but all we have left. Thus, with grateful hearts, we thank you for this food. As it sustains our bodies, we pray we may experience your sustaining power in our hearts and spirits also, renewing courage and making us strong. In Christ's name we ask. Amen.

✣

AFTER THE FUNERAL
OF A LOVED ONE

Blessed are all thy saints, O God and King, who have traveled over the tempestuous sea of this life, and have made the harbor of peace and felicity. Watch over us who are still in our dangerous voyage and remember such as lie exposed to the rough storms of trouble and temptations. Frail is our vessel, and the ocean is wide; but, as in thy mercy thou hast set our course, so steer the vessel of our life toward the everlasting shore of peace, and bring us at length to the quiet haven of our hearts' desire, where thou, O our God, art blessed and livest and reignest forever and ever. Amen.

AUGUSTINE

✦

WHEN SOMEONE HAS LEFT HOME

Our Father, for many years you have cared
for our family. We thank you. For our
absent loved ones now we ask your loving
kindness. Protect them. Keep them honorable.
Grant that we may be worthy of their love.
For Christ's sake let them not be embarrassed
because of us nor us because of them. Grant
us courage to endure minor troubles and
trials and to accept death, loss and
disappointment as if they were straws upon
the tide of life. Amen.

ROBERT LOUIS STEVENSON *(Adapted)*

✤

WHEN SOMEONE RETURNS HOME

Lord, we're all together at home once more.
We thank you for protecting ————
when *(he* or *she)* was gone. We thank you
that you watch over and protect each one
of us as we leave home every day. You are
with us on the freeways in our cars and
busses, on bicycles, on foot, and flying in
planes, as we move about in city and country,
at school, home, and place of work. We can
never go beyond the circle of your care. We
know this is true even if misfortune should
strike us. We praise and thank you that once
again you have spared us from accidents,
especially ———— who has been gone from
our home. Thank you, Father, that once
again our family can join hands and break
bread together. We praise and worship you.
In Christ's name, Amen.

✤

FAMILY CELEBRATION

As we come together
may Thy blessings rest
on this group, O Father,
on each welcome guest.
Give us joy in service.
Grant that we may see
when we help each other
that we are serving Thee. Amen.

✤

BIRTHDAY

Father, we thank you for ―――― whose
birthday we are celebrating. You gave life in
the beginning. You have continued to nourish
and sustain that life. We praise and thank
you. Be with _____ this coming year,
quicken *(his* or *her)* enthusiasm for living,
comfort *(him* or *her)* when disappointments
come, cheer *(him* or *her)* when success
rewards, raise *(him* or *her)* up when *(he* or
she) falls, encourage *(him* or *her)* when the
days are difficult. May your peace, love, joy,
and hope abide in *(his* or *her)* heart today
and always. Amen.

✤

ANNIVERSARY

Our Father, the years have sped by and here
we are, celebrating another anniversary.
We want to thank you first of all for all your
goodness. Life has presented us with joy and
sorrow, adventure and routine, success and
failure, satisfaction and disappointment,
abundance and need, friends and enemies.
Through it all you have never failed us.
We have never gone naked or hungry or
homeless. Nor have we felt completely
forsaken, unloved, or unwanted. Your grace
has given us also peace of heart, assurance
of forgiveness, purpose for living, and a hope
beyond the grave. How rich we are, Father!
Accept our humble thanks. In gratitude we
pledge ourselves anew not to hold our lives
too important, so we may finish our race and
complete the assignment you have given us
to tell others the good news about your
kindness and love. Amen.

♣

FAMILY REUNIONS

Our heavenly Father, we thank you for this,
our extended family, for the love and support
we draw from each other. We praise you for
your faithfulness to each one of us and for
your faithfulness to our family through the
generations. We offer you our thanks because
you have bounteously provided for all our
needs.

We recall with gratitude the loved ones who
used to gather with us and sit at table with
us. We thank you for the inspiration which
has come to us through their lives. We pray
that when our time comes to leave this life we
may be found believing and trusting you; in
Christ's name, Amen.

✤